Sight-Read It for Strings

Improving Reading and Sight-Reading Skills in the String Classroom

Andrew Dabczynski, Richard Meyer & Bob Phillips

Violin

Welcome to *Sight-Read It for Strings: Improving Reading and Sight-Reading Skills in the String Classroom or Studio*. This book will help you become better at reading—and specifically, sight reading—music. Here's how:

First, work with your teacher to learn at least one of the systems used to count beats in music (listed on page 3). Then, look at the "Sight Reading Checklist" on page 2, and identify clues that can help you understand how to play unfamiliar music with ease. Next, turn to any unit in the book. Each unit addresses a separate set of sight reading challenges that you will discover as you play the "Pretest." Following the Pretest is a series of exercises that will help you to practice and focus on each of these issues. Once you can easily play these exercises, sight read the "Post Test." After the Post Test is a "Special" page that explores other music reading concepts. Finally, each unit closes with an ensemble piece that you can play with your friends that revisits all of that unit's sight reading challenges. As you practice through this book, your ability to read music will get stronger and stronger! Good luck, and get ready to get reading!

table of contents

sight reading checklist

Before playing a piece of music for the first time, look it over carefully for these important clues which will make sight-reading the piece easier and more successful. Make sure you take time to think about the following:

1. Title
The title may indicate something about the style or mood of the piece.

2. Composer
The composer's name may be a clue to the style of music.

3. Tempo and Tempo Changes
These markings indicate the speed and any speed changes.

4. Key Signature and Key Changes
These indicate which scale notes to play and when they change.

5. Time Signatures and Time Changes
These indicate the meter and when it will change.

6. "Road Map"
These markings indicate where to go in the music and other important visual cues.

If you have time you should also check the following items:

7. Beginning and Ending Dynamics
The dynamics tell you how loud or soft to play at the beginning and end of the piece.

8. Accidentals
These indicate when pitches are altered in some way.

9. Articulations
Articulation markings indicate the length of the notes and special ways to use the bow.

Now use this checklist to guide you as you look over the piece below. Discuss the process with your teacher and classmates, then play the piece.

1 Surprise Symphony

Franz Joseph Haydn (1732–1809)

counting systems

When sight-reading music, it is important to be able to count the rhythms in the music out loud, then silently "in your head." Musicians use a variety of different systems to count rhythms. In three common systems, students speak (1) beat numbers, (2) syllables (such as the Gordon System) or (3) beat numbers and syllables (as in the McHose System).

Read the rhythm examples below, using each system (or one suggested by your teacher) to count the beats. Be sure to whisper the beats in parentheses.

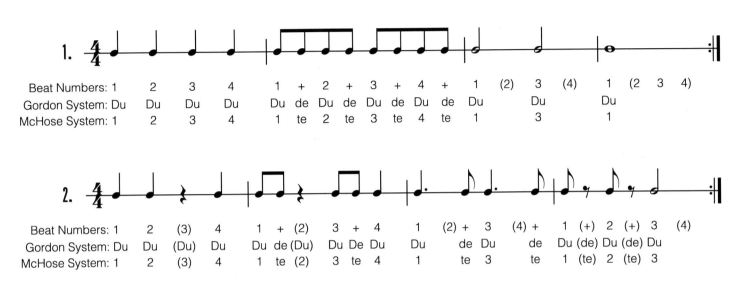

Beat Numbers:	1	2	3	4	1	+	2	+	3	+	4	+	1	(2)	3	(4)	1	(2 3 4)
Gordon System:	Du	Du	Du	Du	Du	de	Du	de	Du	de	Du	de	Du		Du		Du	
McHose System:	1	2	3	4	1	te	2	te	3	te	4	te	1		3		1	

Beat Numbers:	1	2	(3)	4	1	+	(2)	3	+	4	1	(2)	+	3	(4)	+	1	(+) 2 (+) 3 (4)
Gordon System:	Du	Du	(Du)	Du	Du	de	(Du)	Du	De	Du	Du		de	Du		de	Du	(de) Du (de) Du
McHose System:	1	2	(3)	4	1	te	(2)	3	te	4	1		te	3		te	1	(te) 2 (te) 3

Students use other counting systems, too. Whatever system you use, it is important to use a counting system consistently.

Using the system your teacher suggests:

1. Count the following rhythm exercises out loud. Clap or tap a steady beat as you count.
2. Write what you spoke under the beats as you repeat the exercises silently, (syllables or numbers).
3. Play the rhythms using a note of your choice, or notes suggested by your teacher.

Hot Shot Challenge: Can you play the rhythms on one note and count out loud at the same time?

Unit 1 dotted quarters and eighth notes

Play each exercise using a dynamic suggested by your teacher.

Pre-Test

Dotted Quarter Notes on Beat Three

8.

Dotted Quarter Notes on Beat Two

9.

Slurred Dotted Quarter/Eighth

10.

Hooked Dotted Quarter/Eighth

11.

Post-Test

12.

Hot Shot Challenge: Try counting a steady beat out loud while you play all of the exercises in Unit 1.

unit 1 special "road maps"

Count, clap, and then play the exercises below on a note of your choice:

Repeat Sign:
Repeat to the begining

Repeat Sign:
Repeat to the left-facing repeat

1st and 2nd Endings
Repeat to the left repeat, play through and skip to the second ending

D.C. al Fine *(Da Capo al Fine)* Go back to the beginning and play to the *Fine* (end).

D.S. al Fine *(Dal Segno al Fine)* Go back to the sign (𝄋) and play to the *Fine.*

D.C. al Coda *(Da Capo al Coda)*
Go back to the beginning, play to the *"to Coda"* sign, then jump to the *Coda* (⊕) to finish the piece.

D.S. al Coda *(Dal Segno al Coda)*
Go back to the sign, play to the *"to Coda"* sign, then jump to the *Coda* to finish the piece.

"road maps" special — before playing, look over the "road map" so you know where you're going!

Hot Shot Challenge: To play an example of *D.S. al Fine* go back to page 2 and play "Surprise Symphony" again.

Men of Harlech March

Traditional British
Arr. by Richard Meyer

unit 2   long notes

Play each exercise using a dynamic suggested by your teacher.

Pre-Test

Long Notes and Quarter Notes

Long Notes and Eighth Notes

Half Notes, Dotted Half Notes and Whole Notes

Dotted Half Notes and Whole Notes

Post-Test

Hot Shot Challenge: Add your own dynamic markings to the pre-test and post-test.
Play the exercises again, this time with your dynamics.

unit 2 special subdividing

Subdividing long notes into quarter notes:

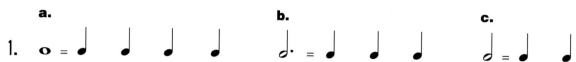

1.

Subdividing long notes into eighth notes:

2.

On the empty staff below, write these long notes in *quarter note* subdivisions, then play your new exercise.
(The first measure is completed for you)

3.

On the empty staff below, write a new exercise, subdividing into *eighth notes*. Play your new exercise.

4.

Play this exercise as written. Without writing it out, play it again while subdividing each note into *quarter notes*.

5.

Without writing it out, play this line while subdividing each note into *eighth notes*.

6.

Hot Shot Challenge: Go back to pages 8 & 9 ("Long Notes") and play those exercises
by subdividing into 1) *quarter notes* and 2) *eighth notes*.

Theme from Symphony No. 1

Gustav Mahler (1860–1911)
Arr. by Bob Phillips

Melody

Accompaniment

unit 3 rests

Play each exercise using a dynamic suggested by your teacher.

Pre-Test

1.

Quarter Notes with Quarter and Half Rests

2.

Quarter and Half Notes with Quarter, Half, and Whole Rests

3.

Whole, Dotted Half, Half, and Quarter Notes with Quarter and Half Rests

4.

Quarter and Dotted Half Notes with Quarter, Half, and Whole Rests

5.

Eighth Notes with Quarter and Whole Rests

Half, Quarter, and Eighth Notes with Quarter and Whole Rests

Half and Eighth Notes with Quarter and Whole Rests

Half Rests and Whole Rests

Post-Test

Hot Shot Challenge: Play the Pre-Test while a friend plays the Post-Test. You'll hear a nice surprise!

unit 3 special   dynamics

Dynamics are symbols that indicate how loud or soft to play, and are traditionaly written in Italian.

Write in the definitions for the following dynamic markings (you may wish to use the glossary on page 47 of *String Explorer Book 1,* if necessary).

f — *forte* _____

mf — *mezzo forte* _____

mp — *mezzo piano* _____

p — *piano* _____

⟨＜＿ crescendo _____

⟩＞＿ decrescendo _____

cresc. — crescendo _____

dim. — diminuendo _____

Different dynamics are produced by changing:

    (1) the amount of arm weight used to keep the bow on the string;

    (2) the speed of the bow;

    (3) the distance from the bridge that the bow is placed on the string.

Use these three ideas as you perform the exercises below, playing the rhythms on a single note.

Play the following exercises, using the ideas above to create dynamic changes.

Theme and Variation on "Spring"

Theme by Antonio Vivaldi (1678–1741)
Arr. by Andrew Dabczynski

Melody

Accompaniment

unit 4 ties

Pre-Test

Quarter Notes Tied to Eighth Notes

Quarter Notes Tied to Half, Dotted Half, and Whole Notes

Half Notes Tied to Eighth and Quarter Notes

Half Notes Tied to Half and Dotted Half Notes

5.

Dotted Half Notes Tied to Half and Dotted Half Notes

6.

Dotted Half Notes Tied to Eighth Notes

7.

Half Notes Tied to Eighth Notes

8.

Half Notes Tied to Quarter Notes

9.

Post-Test

10.

Hot Shot Challenge: Play the exercises on pages 16–17 again as if there are no ties.
Be careful: the bowings may now be different than marked!

unit 4 special   meter changes and conducting

Your teacher will show you how to conduct each beat pattern. Try conducting each line below.

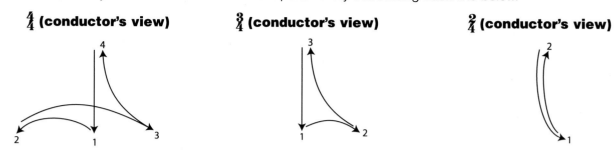

Conducting Patterns

Play the famous melodies below. Try to identify the title and composer of each. Then practice following the conductor by:

1. Playing only the down beat notes while watching the conductor.
2. Playing all the notes, making sure to look up at the conductor at each change of tempo.

Meter Changes—On the pieces below:

1. Circle the downbeats
2. Play the downbeat notes only.
3. Play the entire exercise.
4. Play the piece and look up at the conductor for a moment every time you play a downbeat.
5. Take turns with your friends conducting each exercise.

Mixed-Up Bach

Themes by J.S. Bach (1685–1750)
Arr. by Bob Phillips

Melody

Accompaniment

unit 5 note values: long to short / short to long

Eighth Notes to Dotted Half Notes

Dotted Quarters/Eighth Notes to Half Notes

Dotted Quarters/Eighth Notes to Whole Notes

Post-Test

10

Hot Shot Challenge: Play the Pre-Test and Post-Test again, this time with subdivision. Substitute the correct number of quarter notes for every whole note, dotted-half note, and half note that you see. Be careful—the bowings may be different from those that are printed!

unit 5 special bowings and articulations

Play the following lines, being sure to observe the bowings, articulations, and lift signs.

Practice the following exercises using slurs and hooked bowings. Write in up-bow marks over each hooked bowing.

What symbol is used to indicate that a note is played pizzicato with the left hand? _____

What symbol is used to indicate that a note is played with an accent, or bite, of the bow? _____

Practice the following exercises using strong accents and left hand pizzicato where marked.

Noel's Galliard

Melody

Anthony Holborne (?)
Arr. by Andrew Dabczynski

unit 6   conjunct (stepwise) interval patterns

Pre-Test

Try to train your eyes so you recognize the direction of the patterns at a glance.

Conjunct Pattern No. 1

Conjunct Pattern No. 2

Conjunct Pattern No. 3

4.

Conjunct Pattern Nos. 1 & 3

5.

Conjunct Pattern Nos. 1 & 2

6.

Post-Test

7.

Hot Shot Challenge: Throughout the Post-Test, identify patterns 1, 2, or 3 by drawing the correct shape over each group of eighth notes. Refer to Exercises 2, 3, and 4 to review how each shape is drawn, then play the Post-Test again.

unit 6 special accompaniment patterns

For each of the following accompaniment patterns: 1. Count; 2. Clap or tap; 3. Play on the note of your choice.

Divide the players into two teams. Have Team 1 play the following accompaniment pattern while Team 2 plays the D Major scale *with two half notes for each pitch*. Then, switch parts.

Divide the players into two teams. Have Team 1 play the following accompaniment pattern while Team 2 plays the D Major scale *with one dotted-half note for each pitch*. Then, switch parts.

Divide the players into two teams. Have Team 1 play the following accompaniment pattern while Team 2 plays the D Major scale *with one half note for each pitch*. Then, switch parts.

Old Joe Clark

Traditional American
Arr. by Richard Meyer

Melody

Accompaniment

unit 7 disjunct (skipping) interval patterns

Pre-Test

1.

Tonic (I) Arpeggio D-F♯-A

2.

Sub-Dominant (IV) Arpeggio G-B-D

3.

Dominant Seventh (V⁷) Arpeggio A-C♯-E-G

4.

A Simple Chord Progression

Intervals of a Sixth

Post-Test

Hot Shot Challenge: Write the correct chord symbol (**I, IV, V7**) in the boxes of the Post-Test.
Discuss your answers with your teacher, then play the exercise again.

unit 7 special   accidentals and key changes

Bugle-Call Blues

Richard Meyer (b.1957)

E + C string special

1.

2.

3.

4.

5.

6.